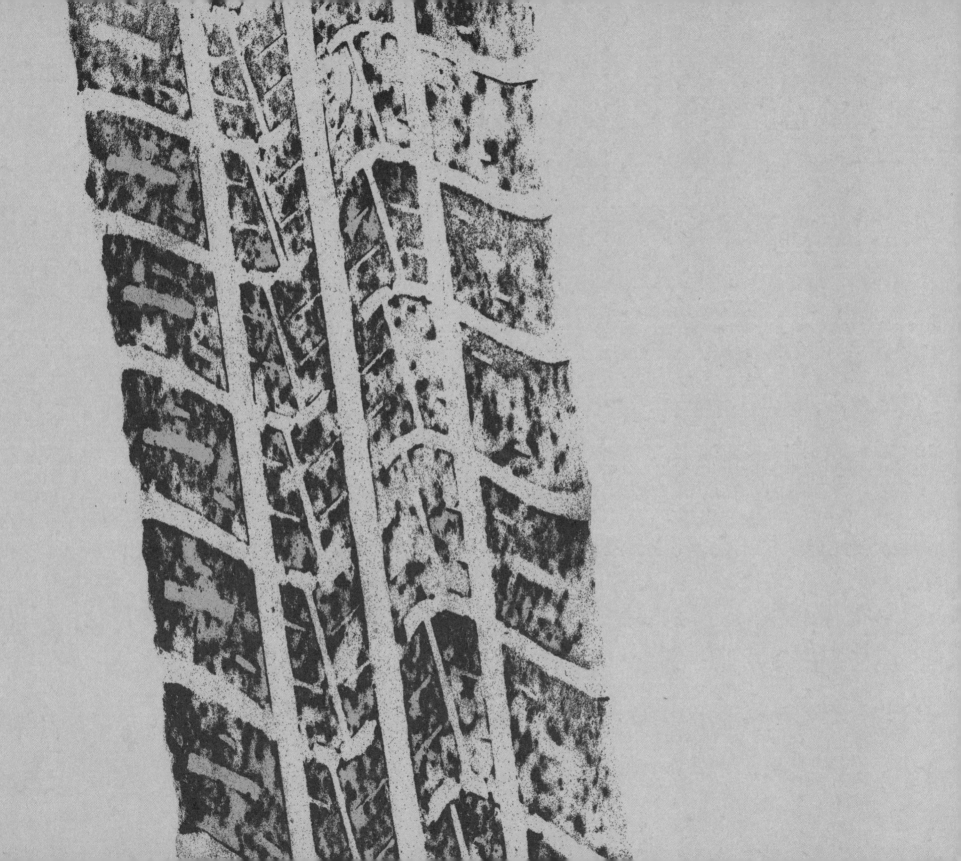

I DRIVE A FIRE ENGINE

by **Sarah Bridges**

illustrated by **Amy Bailey Muehlenhardt**

PICTURE WINDOW BOOKS
Minneapolis, Minnesota

Thank you to Sarah Larson and Mark Kuhnly of the Golden Valley
Fire Department for sharing their extensive fire knowledge. S.B.

Editor: Jill Kalz
Designer: Jaime Martens
Page Production: Tracy Kaehler
Creative Director: Keith Griffin
Editorial Director: Carol Jones
The illustrations in this book were created digitally.

Picture Window Books
5115 Excelsior Boulevard
Suite 232
Minneapolis, MN 55416
877-845-8392
www.picturewindowbooks.com

Library of Congress Cataloging-in-Publication Data
Bridges, Sarah.
I drive a fire engine / by Sarah Bridges ; illustrated by
Amy Bailey Muehlenhardt.
p. cm. — (Working wheels)
Includes bibliographical references and index.
ISBN 1-4048-1606-2 (hardcover)
1. Fire engines—Juvenile literature. 2. Fire extinction—Juvenile literature. 3. Fire
fighters—Juvenile literature. I. Muehlenhardt, Amy Bailey, 1974- ill. II. Title.
TH9372.B75 2006
628.9'259—dc22   2005023141

Thanks to our advisers for their expertise,
research, and advice:

Roger E. Kalz, Volunteer Firefighter
New Ulm (Minnesota) Fire Department

Susan Kesselring, M.A., Literacy Educator
Rosemount—Apple Valley—Eagan
(Minnesota) School District

My name is Jackson. I drive a fire engine. Fire engines are special kinds of fire trucks. They pump water to put out fires. They're also called pumpers.

There are two other kinds of fire trucks: the tanker and the ladder. The tanker carries water. The ladder truck helps firefighters reach tall places.

5

When my pager beeps, I know there's an emergency. I race to put on my turnout gear. It includes fire-resistant pants, thick boots, a heavy coat, and a helmet.

Before fire truck drivers leave the station, they check maps. They need to make sure they know where the emergency is.

I jump into my cab and start the engine. Other firefighters jump on the fire engine, too. I turn on the flashing lights and drive out of the station. The siren howls. As I approach a busy street, I honk the horn.

The law says that cars have to pull over to the side of the road when a fire truck is coming. This lets firefighters get to an emergency more quickly.

9

When I arrive at a fire, I connect one hose from the pumper to the hydrant. I connect another hose from the pumper to a nozzle. Water flows from the hydrant, into the pumper, and out through the nozzle.

Most fire hydrants are painted red, with different colored caps. The colors tell firefighters how much water flows out of the hydrants. Red hydrants are the slowest. Blue-green hydrants are the fastest.

Soon, the other fire trucks arrive.
If the fire is big, or if there are no
hydrants, the tanker truck dumps its
water into a portable pool. The pumper
sucks up water from this pool. It can
also pump water from lakes or rivers.

ENGINE
COMPAN

Dials on the side of the pumper show how much water the engine is pumping.

A hose full of pumping water is heavy and hard to control. It takes two or more firefighters to hold it. My partner and I point the nozzle at the base of the flames.

Some firefighters go into smoky buildings to rescue people or animals. They wear masks and air tanks to help them breathe.

After the fire is out,
I fold the hoses back
on the fire engine.
The hoses are stored
in the hose bed.

KEEP BACK

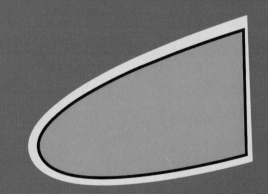

The average pumper can pump up to 1,250 gallons (4,750 liters) of water every minute. That amount is equal to 20,000 glasses of water!

Some fire stations have front and back garage doors. Firefighters drive their trucks in one door and out the other. At stations with just front doors, drivers must back their trucks into the garage.

Back at the station,
I check the pumper's
water tank. I refill it
if the water level is
low. I also refill the
gas tank.

All of the firefighters help clean the trucks. We also clean our turnout gear and any tools we used. After everything is put away, I close the garage doors and wait for the next emergency.

Fire trucks must be ready to go at any time and in any kind of weather.

FIRE ENGINE DIAGRAM

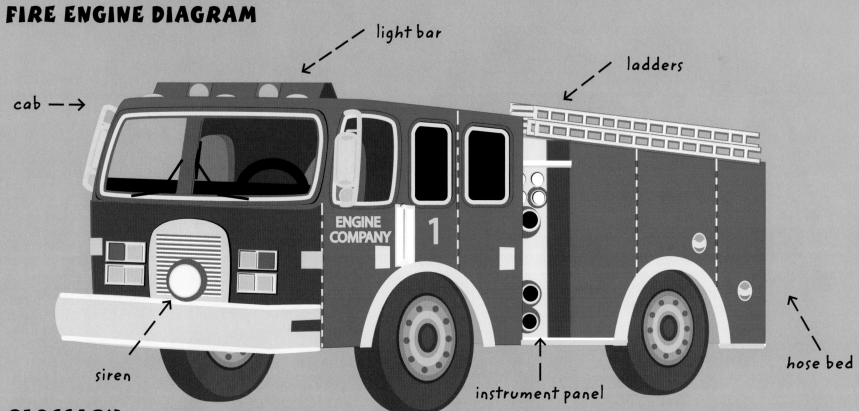

light bar

ladders

cab →

siren

instrument panel

hose bed

ENGINE COMPANY 1

GLOSSARY

cab—the front of a fire truck where the driver sits

fire-resistant—will not burn easily

hydrant—a metal cap covering a big, underground water pipe; firefighters pump water from a hydrant to fight fires

nozzle—a heavy metal tube that attaches to a water hose

pager—a small electronic box that receives messages; also called a beeper

portable—can be carried or moved

turnout gear—the special clothing worn by firefighters

FUN FACTS

 At the beginning of the 1900s, there were no fire trucks. Horse-drawn wagons brought firefighters to the scene of a fire.

 The first fire trucks were built in 1913, five years after the first car was made.

 Long fire trucks have two cabs and two drivers. One driver sits in the front cab, and the other driver sits in the back cab. The back cab is called a tillerman's cab. A "tillerman" is someone who steers.

 Firefighters keep their turnout gear in ready position at all times. The legs of their pants are always resting around their boots. All firefighters have to do is stick their feet in their boots and pull their pants up.

TO LEARN MORE

At the Library

Gordon, Sharon. *What's Inside a Fire Truck?*
New York: Benchmark Books, 2004.

Simon, Seymour. *Fighting Fires.* New York:
SeaStar Books, 2002.

Teitelbaum, Michael. *If I Could Drive a
Fire Truck.* New York: Scholastic, 2001.

On the Web

FactHound offers a safe, fun way to find Internet sites
related to this book. All of the sites on FactHound
have been researched by our staff.

1. Visit www.facthound.com

2. Type in this special code
   for age-appropriate sites:
   1404816062

3. Click on the FETCH IT button.

Your trusty FactHound will fetch the best sites for you!

INDEX

LOOK FOR ALL OF THE BOOKS IN THE WORKING WHEELS SERIES:

- I Drive a Backhoe
  1-4048-1604-6
- I Drive a Bulldozer
  1-4048-0613-X
- I Drive a Crane
  1-4048-1605-4
- I Drive a Dump Truck
  1-4048-0614-8

- I Drive a Fire Engine
  1-4048-1606-2
- I Drive a Freight Train
  1-4048-1607-0
- I Drive a Garbage Truck
  1-4048-0615-6
- I Drive an Ambulance
  1-4048-0618-0

- I Drive a Semitruck
  1-4048-0616-4
- I Drive a Snowplow
  1-4048-0617-2
- I Drive a Street Sweeper
  1-4048-1608-9
- I Drive a Tractor
  1-4048-1609-7

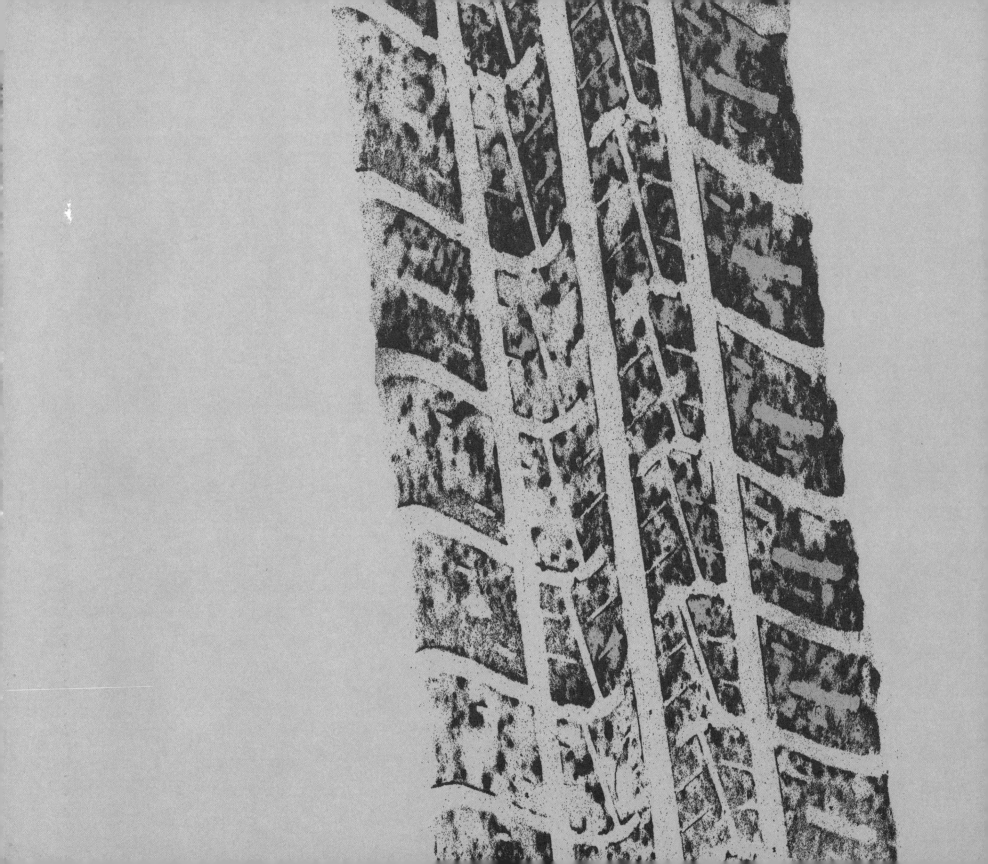